# ANNE
# FRANK
## Her Life

First published in the UK in 2010 by
Evans Brothers Ltd
2A Portman Mansions
Chiltern Street
London W1U 6NR
www.evansbooks.co.uk

Reprinted 2011, 2012

British Library Cataloguing in Publication Data
A catalogue record for this book is available from the British Library.

ISBN-13: 9780237539245

Printed by Everbest Printing Company Ltd, China.
in October 2011, Job number 1694

Photos © family photos Anne Frank: AFF, Basel/AFS, Amsterdam; Anne
Frank Stichting Amsterdam, www.annefrank.org; AFS/Allard Bovenberg;
USHMM, Washington/Mark Chrzanowski; Maria Austria Institute;
Netherlands Institute for War Documentation, Amsterdam;
Imperial War Museum, London

*Anne Frank – Her Life* has been written in simple, easy-to-read English.
Some quotations have been simplified, and the narrative does not always
follow the order of events in Anne Frank's diary. The photographs of the
rooms in the secret annex were taken when it was furnished temporarily
for a film.

The Anne Frank Trust UK runs exhibitions and education programmes.
www.annefrank.org.uk

# ANNE FRANK
## Her Life

MARIAN HOEFNAGEL

NARRATIVE TEXT TRANSLATED BY
ROBIN PASCOE

Evans

# Introduction

During the Second World War the German leader, Adolf Hitler, ordered his Nazi followers to round up people they considered to be 'inferior'. The people the Nazis hated most were Jews, and millions of them were sent to prison camps, called concentration camps. The conditions there were terrible. Thousands died of disease or starvation, but most of them were murdered in gas chambers by the Nazis. Many Jews went into hiding, helped by brave people who risked their own freedom. Often, though, they were betrayed by Hitler's supporters. Like Anne Frank's family, these Jews were sent to concentration camps, where most of them died. By the end of the war, more than six million Jews had been killed, 1.5 million of them children like Anne.

# Anne

On 12 June 1929, a little girl is born in Germany. She is a happy girl – she has a mother and father who love her, and a sister who is mad about her. She lives in a beautiful city: Frankfurt am Main. Lots of her relations live there too. They all come to look at the little girl, and everyone likes her.

The girl is called Anne – Annelies Marie Frank – an ordinary name. At that moment, no one knows her life will be short. No one knows she will never be older than 15. No one knows she will become famous all over the world. But that is what happens.

Little Anne is a nice baby and a funny toddler. She is very different from her older sister Margot, who is quiet and does what her mother says. Anne talks a lot and asks lots of questions.

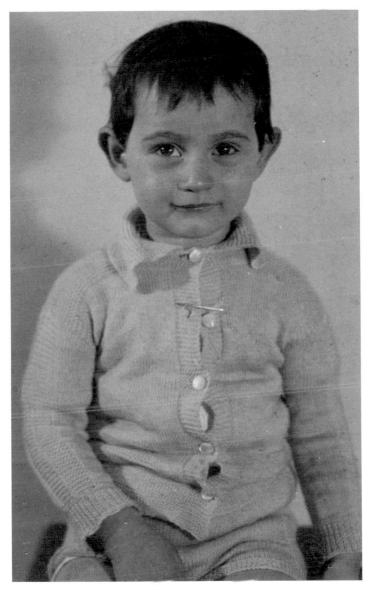

**Anne Frank at two years old**
*Anne is a happy little girl.*

# Tension

Anne and Margot have a good life. Lots of children live nearby and they play together every day. They do not know that their parents are worried – very worried. The Frank family owns a bank and lots of members of the family work at the bank, including Anne's father. It is not a big bank, but it has made the family rich. However, now the bank is not doing so well.

The Frank family bank is not the only one in trouble. All the banks in Germany are having difficulties, as are all the factories and all the shops. Things are not going well in Germany. The country is in crisis and many people do not have jobs.

But there is something else worrying Anne's parents – Germany's new leader. He is called

*Anne (third from left) and Margot (fourth from right)*
*The sisters enjoy playing with the neighbourhood children.*

Adolf Hitler and he hates Jews.
He blames them for Germany's troubles.
That is nonsense, of course, but many
Germans think Hitler is right and that
the Jews have caused the crisis, so they
don't like Jews either.

Hitler's supporters are called Nazis, and
they make life very difficult for the Jews in
Germany. There are laws against Jews.

Suddenly, many Jews are not allowed to work for the council or as teachers. They lose their jobs. Jewish children are put into separate groups at school, and they are bullied by their classmates. The Frank family, which is Jewish, has difficulties as well.

*Adolf Hitler in Nuremberg, Germany, 1927*
*Hitler's party starts small, but it gets more and more supporters.*

# A New Life

Anne's parents decide to leave Germany.
They want to go to the Netherlands (also
called Holland), to Amsterdam, because the
Netherlands does not have a dictator like
Hitler. In the Netherlands, Jews have the
same rights as other people.

Anne's father starts a company in
Amsterdam called Opekta, which sells
a product needed to make jam. Anne's
mother and father move to Amsterdam
first. Anne and Margot stay with their
grandmother in Germany for a little while.

Anne's father starts working at Opekta
and Anne's mother looks for a house for
the family to live in. It is not always easy to
find a house in Amsterdam but luckily, new
houses have been built in the south of the

city. Anne's mother finds a house there, on Merwede Square, which means that the girls can come to Amsterdam.

Margot arrives first. She is seven years old and has to go to school. Little Anne is three and stays a while longer with her grandmother in Germany. A couple of months later, she comes to the Netherlands as well – on Margot's birthday. She is put on the table like a present.

'Happy birthday, Margot,' say her father and mother. 'This is your present.' It is the best present of the day. The family is together again.

'We have our life back,' says Anne's father. 'We are safe here. We are free. We are making a new start in the Netherlands.'

Anne's family is safely together again, but Anne's mother misses Germany and her family. She does not know many people in the Netherlands, and she can't speak Dutch. Her husband works long hours at Opekta because the company is new and takes up a lot of his time. Mrs Frank is alone a lot, especially when the girls are at school. Margot goes to primary school and Anne already goes to kindergarten.

*Anne and Margot in Aachen, Germany*
*This photograph was taken while they were staying with their grandmother, just before they moved to the Netherlands.*

# Becoming Dutch

More and more people from Germany come and live in the same neighbourhood. They are German Jews, like the Frank family, who have all fled Hitler. They are all frightened by the Nazis' hatred of Jews.

Mr and Mrs Frank make new friends quickly, and Margot and Anne make lots of friends as well, friends who live near them and friends from school. Nearly all of them are Jewish and nearly all of them are German.

Anne and Margot learn Dutch quickly, because they hear it all day long. They speak Dutch with their German friends as well. What they really want is just to be ordinary Dutch people.

'My mother and father speak really bad Dutch,' says one of Margot's friends. 'I have

to correct them all the time. It's embarrassing.'
The children from Germany think it is
important to be Dutch. That is why Margot's
friend won't wear German clothes – no
puffed sleeves, no aprons and little jackets –
because then you can see from miles away
they are German, and they don't want that
at all.

Margot is good at school – she always
gets high marks – but Anne is not such a
good pupil. She always chats and laughs with
her friends, and does not spend enough time
listening. But she can tell good stories. She
often thinks up the stories with her father.

'I want to be a writer when I grow up,'
she tells her teacher. That wish comes true.
A few years later she begins keeping her
diary, and it becomes the most famous diary
in the world.

# Is It Allowed?

On the night of 10 May 1940, the German army attacks the Netherlands. Hitler had promised he would not do so, which is why the Jews felt safe in the Netherlands. That feeling ends in just one night. Lots of Jews kill themselves that day – they are frightened of what the Nazis are planning. Of course, Anne's parents are frightened as well.

At first, though, not much changes in their day-to-day lives. Anne and Margot go to school. Their father works hard at Opekta. Their mother does the housekeeping.

But then come the laws for Jews.

```
Jews have to wear a Star of David.
Jews have to hand over their bikes.
Jews are not allowed in the tram.
```

Jews are not allowed to drive cars.

Jews can only go shopping between
　　3.00 p.m. and 5.00 p.m. and only
　　in Jewish shops.

Jews are not allowed on the streets
　　after 8.00 p.m. and cannot sit in
　　their gardens.

Jews can't go to the theatre or the cinema.

Jews can only go to a Jewish hairdresser.

Jews can't take part in sports.

Jews can't go swimming or play tennis
　　or hockey.

Jews can't visit Christians at home.

Jews have to go to Jewish schools.

And so it goes on...

Anne, too, has trouble with all the laws for Jews. In the summer, she is not allowed to go to the swimming pool. In the winter she is not allowed to go to the ice rink. That really makes her unhappy because she has just got new skates and she loves skating.

And so life goes on. Jews can't do this and can't do that. Anne's friend Jacqueline says: 'I don't dare to do anything any more because I am afraid it's not allowed.'

One day, Anne's parents hear that all the Jews have to go back to Germany. It is only a rumour, but it worries Anne's parents. They don't tell their daughters – they don't want to frighten Anne and Margot.

# The Diary

On Friday, 12 June 1942, Anne wakes up at
six in the morning. Of course, she knows why:
it is her birthday and she is 13 years old. She
stays in bed until 6.45 a.m., but she can't wait
any longer. She goes to the sitting room and
sees all her presents on the table. There are
lots of presents, but the best of all is a diary.

**The diary**
*Anne gets a diary for her 13th birthday. It becomes her best friend.*

Anne thinks her diary should become her friend, a friend she can tell everything to. She does not have a friend like that. She calls the friend Kitty, and Anne often starts a diary entry with 'Dear Kitty'.

Anne writes in her diary straight away.

*'I hope I will be able to confide everything to you, as I have never been able to confide in anyone, and I hope you will be a great source of comfort and support.'*

Then she writes about her family and about the children in her class at school. She also writes that she is looking forward to the summer holidays. But her carefree life is about to change.

On 5 July a letter from the SS arrives for Margot. She has to report for work in Germany, and if she does not the entire family will be taken prisoner. Anne can't believe it. Margot is just 16! Young girls like her should not be sent to Germany all alone. Anne cries. The troubles brought by the war are getting very close.

**Margot Frank**
*Margot is just 16 when she gets a message from the SS saying she has to report for work in Germany.*

# Gone

One thing is clear – Margot will not go to
Germany. The Frank family will go into
hiding immediately. Margot and Anne are
in a state, but they begin putting their things
into their satchels.

The first thing Anne packs is her diary,
and then schoolbooks, curlers, old letters,
hankies and a comb. 'Will we really go into
hiding?' she asks herself. 'In the city, in the
country, in a house, a hut, how, where?'
Anne has no idea.

*'I stuck the craziest things in the satchel,'*
she writes later in her diary.

That evening Miep Gies, who works for
Opekta, and her husband Jan visit the
family. They take shoes, dresses, coats,
underwear and stockings to the secret

address. The Frank family can't carry suitcases through the streets because German soldiers would think they are trying to escape.

It is late when Anne finally goes to bed. She knows it will be her last night in her own bed but she still falls asleep straight away.

The next day a warm rain is falling, but they still put on lots of clothes.

'It is as if we are going off to spend the night in a fridge,' writes Anne.

She is wearing two vests, three pairs of pants, a skirt, a dress, a jacket, a raincoat, two pairs of stockings, heavy shoes, a cap and a scarf. She finds it hard to breathe, but it is the only way to take clothes with them.

They leave the breakfast things on the table. They strip the beds. It is as if they left in a hurry. They leave some food for Anne's cat, Moortje, and a letter for the neighbour asking him to take care of her.

Anne and her parents walk through the pouring rain. Miep Gies has already picked up Margot by bike and gone on ahead. Anne and her parents are each carrying a satchel and a very full shopping bag. Now Anne finally hears about the plan to go into hiding. Her parents had been planning to go into hiding on 16 July, but Margot's call-up means they are moving 10 days earlier, which is why their secret hiding place is not yet ready.

They go into hiding in the middle of Amsterdam, on a street called the Prinsengracht, where Anne's father's business Opekta is. The back part of the building is not used and that is where Anne's father and some friends have been taking food and furniture for some months. This is where Anne will live for more than two years – the secret annex.

# The Secret Annex

The secret annex is a complete mess –
everywhere there are boxes waiting to
be unpacked. Anne's mother and Margot
lie down on the unmade beds. They feel
so awful.

Anne and her father want to start tidying
up straight away, but first they have to make
curtains otherwise the neighbours can see in.
They sew scraps of material together and
pin them to the window frames. Then they
unpack the boxes and put everything away
in cupboards; then they clean the floor. By
evening they are still not finished, but at
least everyone can sleep in a clean bed.

The next day, they keep going from early
morning to late at night, and finally everything
is ready. They can't go out and do the shopping

so Miep buys the groceries. They all eat together in the secret annex for the first time.

Anne is very pleased with their hiding place. *'There's probably not a more comfortable hiding place in all of Amsterdam. No. In all of Holland,'* she writes.

The annex is quite big. Downstairs is a bed-sitting room for Anne's parents, Anne and Margot's room, and a room with a toilet and a wash basin. Anne cheers up the room straight away. With glue, she sticks up film-star photographs, postcards and pictures from magazines on the wall. It looks much more cheerful.

Upstairs is a big living room and bedroom with a kitchen, which is to be Mr and Mrs Van Pels's room. They are going to hide in the annex as well and are bringing their son Peter, who will get a little room next to the steps to the attic.

Anne finds it strange to have gone into hiding.

'It is more like being on holiday in some sort of boarding house,' she writes.

It is an odd way to look at life in hiding but that, she writes, is how things are.

**The Frank family in 1941**
*This picture was taken a year before they went into hiding.*

# Afraid

Five people who work at Opekta know there are people hiding in the annex: Johannes Kleiman, Miep Gies, Victor Kugler, and Bep Voskuijl and her father Johan Voskuijl. Bep's father works in the storeroom. The other men who work there know nothing, so the people in hiding have to be careful. They have to talk quietly and not make any other noise.

At lunchtime the men in the warehouse have a break, and then the family can eat lunch together. Often some of their helpers eat with them, and in the evenings and at weekends they can go their own way. This is when the people in the annex go downstairs, because in the office there is a radio. They listen together to Radio Oranje, transmitted from England. Radio Oranje

**Some of the Opekta workers in 1941**
*From left to right: Victor Kugler, Esther, Bep Voskuijl, Pine and Miep Gies. Esther and Pine's surnames are unknown – by 1942 they no longer worked at Opekta.*

tells them what is happening in the war.
Of course, you are not allowed to listen to it,
and Anne thinks it is a bit frightening to do
so. She is afraid they will be discovered. She
is afraid she will be shot.

Anne is frightened at night as well. She is frightened of thunder, of gunfire and planes. She's happiest crawling into her father's bed.

*'I know it sounds childish,'* she writes in her diary. *'But wait until it happens to you! The ack-ack guns make so much noise you can't hear your own voice.'*

Anne likes the chiming of the Westertoren clock, though. The Westertoren is almost next to their house on the Prinsengracht, so the family can hear it easily. The bells chime every 15 minutes.

*'It is so reassuring. Especially at night,'* Anne writes.

# A Real Hiding Place

A week later, the Van Pels family arrives:
Hermann, Auguste and their son Peter. Like
the Frank family, they are Jewish and from
Germany. Anne is happy they have arrived.
The silence in the annex makes her nervous
and she thinks it will be much more fun with
other people around.

Peter, who is almost 16, is first to arrive.
Anne thinks he is a shy, dull boy, but she
is happy he has brought his cat, Mouschi.
Anne had to leave her cat behind and she
still misses her a lot.

The Van Pels family bring the Franks up
to date with everything that has happened –
they have been a week longer in the outside

world. 'All your friends think you left suddenly,' Mr Van Pels says. Anne, Margot and their parents think this is very funny. Their plan worked.

In the months that follow there comes bad news – more and more Jews are being called up by the SS. More and more Jews are being sent to Germany to work. If they don't come forward themselves, they are arrested.

To hide the way into the annex, Bep Voskuijl's father builds a big moveable bookcase. He attaches it to the door to the annex so no one can see there is more to the house. Now the annex has become a real hiding place.

**The moveable bookcase**
*Only the helpers and people living in the annex know that the bookcase can open and that there are rooms behind it.*

# Arguments

The people living in the annex are living close together. Because they can't go out, they see each other all day long and they have a lot of rows. Mr and Mrs Van Pels have a lot of arguments. Sometimes they really scream and shout, but Anne says it is usually about nothing.

Mrs Van Pels does not get on with Anne's mother either. They don't scream and shout, but they still bicker. For example, Mrs Van Pels does not like the fact that her plates are always used, not Anne's mother's. She forgets that most of the things in the annex belong to the Frank family and that they use them too.

Mr and Mrs Van Pels criticise Anne a lot as well. They think she is rude and has

*Mr and Mrs Van Pels*
*Mr and Mrs Van Pels and their son Peter went into hiding in the secret annex as well.*

no manners. They think Anne is spoilt and that she should have been brought up better.

'Sir' and 'Madam' really annoy Anne. She thinks they should look at themselves because they don't have any manners. She does not say what she thinks out loud, but she writes it in her diary.

Anne's father usually defends her. 'I think Anne is very well brought up,' he tells Mrs Van Pels one day. 'At least she has learned not to answer you back.'

Anne does not just get irritated by Mr and Mrs Van Pels, she also gets irritated by her mother. Her mother is a lot more patient than 'Sir' and 'Madam', but she still criticises Anne a lot and Anne does not like that. The only person she really loves is her father. She has a pet name for him: Pim. Pim asks Anne to be nicer to her mother and if she can help her more often, but Anne does not plan to do so. Sometimes she gets along well with Margot, but often she thinks Margot is too boring, too quiet and too perfect.

# Reading and Writing

Life in the annex is dull. Of course, household chores still need to be done – washing up, cooking, cleaning, tidying – but they are done quickly. Every day, the people in hiding have a lot of time left to do other things. So they spend their time reading, learning and listening to the radio.

Anne, Margot and Peter have taken schoolbooks with them and try to learn things every day – French, English, history, geography, maths – otherwise they will be behind when they go back to school. Anne likes French and history but she hates maths.

They all read lots as well. Every week Miep brings them five books from the library and they are happy when the new books arrive. Peter and Margot are 16 and are allowed to read all the books, but Anne isn't – her books have to be approved. Anne wants to read books for grown-ups.

When she finally gets hold of one and reads about a girl having her period she writes:

*'I'm probably going to have my period soon. I can tell because I keep finding a whitish smear in my pants... I can hardly wait. It is such a momentous event.'*

But Anne's favourite pastime is writing in her diary. If she feels sad, her diary helps her because when she writes, her sadness disappears. Kitty has really become her best friend. Anne writes:

*'The nicest part is being able to write down all my thoughts and feelings, otherwise I'd absolutely suffocate.'*

# A Newcomer

A new person is to join them in the secret
annex – after all, there is little difference
between seven and eight people. And
outside, the situation for Jews is becoming
more and more dangerous. They want to
help someone else.

Jewish dentist Mr Pfeffer joins them in the
annex. He will sleep in Anne's room instead of
Margot. Margot can sleep on the folding bed
in her parents' room. Mr Pfeffer does not know
what to say when he sees the secret annex, and
he is very surprised to see the Frank family.

'I had heard you left in a hurry,' he says.
'I thought you had gone abroad a long time
ago.' Hermann Van Pels gives him a copy of
the funny rules they have written for living in
the annex.

The Secret Annex: a special place for
  Jews to live in for a while.
Open all year round.
Located in beautiful, quiet surroundings
  in the heart of Amsterdam.
No neighbours.
Price: Free.
Rest hours: from 10.00 p.m. to 7.30 a.m.;
  10.15 a.m. on Sundays.
Use of language: Only the language
  of civilised people may be spoken,
  so no German.

At first Anne likes Mr Pfeffer. She doesn't really like sharing her room, but her father thought it was so important to save someone else, and Anne agrees with her father. But soon she fights with Mr Pfeffer as much as she fights with the other adults. He thinks Anne is rude and noisy, so he often tells her off.

*'This would not be so bad if Mr Pfeffer was not such a tell-tale to Mother,'* she writes.

'Mother lectures me all over again. And if I am really lucky, Mrs Van P calls me to account five minutes later and lays down the law as well. It is not easy being the badly brought-up centre of attention of a family of nit-pickers. In bed at night as I ponder my many sins I get so confused. I either laugh or cry.'

**Fritz Pfeffer**
*At first Anne likes Mr Pfeffer. Later, she often quarrels with him.*

# Bad News

Mr Pfeffer has bad news. Every night military vehicles drive through the city, and soldiers ring every doorbell asking whether any Jews live there. If so, the whole family is taken away; if not, they move on to the next house.

Anne writes:

*'In the evenings, when it is dark, in my thoughts I often see long lines of good, innocent people accompanied by crying children, walking on and on, ordered about by a handful of men who bully and beat them until they nearly drop. No one is spared. The sick, the elderly, children, babies and pregnant women – all are marched to their death. I feel wicked sleeping in a warm bed while somewhere out there my dearest friends are dropping*

*from exhaustion or being knocked to the ground. And all because they are Jews.'*

But still the people in hiding try to have some fun. In 1942, the Jewish festival of Hanukkah falls on 4 December, just one day before the Dutch festival of St Nicholas. They light candles and give each other little presents. And on 5 December, they celebrate St Nicholas, when Dutch children get presents rather than at Christmas. Bep and Miep put a little present and poem for everyone in a basket. Anne likes the St Nicholas party better than Hanukkah.

Worse news comes in from outside: all the Jews found by German soldiers are taken prisoner. They are taken by train to concentration camps.

*'We assume that most of them are being murdered,'* writes Anne. *'The English radio says they are being gassed. Perhaps that's the quickest way to die.'*

# Illness

Anne is worried. Her father is ill: he has a high temperature and is covered in red spots.

*'Just think. We can't even call the doctor,'* she writes.

Anne's mother tries to sweat the fever out, and after a few days his temperature goes down and the strange spots go as well.

*'It is frightening to be ill in the annex,'* writes Anne.

If you have to cough, you have to hide under a blanket, otherwise the people in the warehouse downstairs can hear you, but the tickle does not go away if you cough quietly.

When Anne becomes ill, coughing under the blankets is not the worst thing. The worst thing is her room mate. Mr Pfeffer

**Anne's room**
*Anne has to share her room with Mr Pfeffer. At first she likes him, but later she changes her mind.*

acts as if he is a doctor and listens to her lungs.

*'Then he lays his pomaded head on my bare chest to listen to the sounds,'* writes Anne. *'Not only did his hair tickle but I was embarrassed. Why should he lay his head on my heart? After all, he is not my boyfriend.'*

Anne has also needed glasses for some time – she has to hold books very close to read the letters. Her mother thinks she needs to see an optician. Just think of it – walking down the street! The idea first frightens Anne, but then she is happy. She gets her coat out of the cupboard, but it is far too small.

*'I am curious to see what they decided, only I don't think they'll ever work out a plan,'* she writes.

She's right – it doesn't happen. It would be too dangerous. And the people in hiding think the war will be over soon. But they are wrong about that.

# Fear

The people living in the annex are always
afraid of burglars, not just because they
could lose their things, but because they
could be discovered. And then the burglars
could tell the police.

One night, Mrs Van Pels hears a noise
in the attic. She is worried something has
happened to her son and she wants her
husband to take a look, but he can't be
bothered. 'I'm sure they have not stolen
Peter,' he says. A couple of nights later they
hear the noise again and wake Peter up.
Peter goes to check with a torch. He sees
huge rats eating up their stores. It is easy
to decide what to do. Mouschi has to be put
in the attic. Most rats stay away, but one of
them does bite Peter on his arm.

**The attic of the secret annex**
*The attic is dark and damp, and there are rats.*

Several times they hear noises downstairs. They become very afraid and don't dare to move, but luckily there is never anything to worry about. Until 16 July 1943.

That day Peter goes downstairs to check everything is okay, as he always does – and something is wrong. The outside door is open. Burglars have used an iron bar to break open the outside door. Then they searched the warehouse, but there was not much worth taking, so they went up one floor to the office, where they found some money and cheques, and – much worse – 330 lbs-worth of sugar ration cards.

*'We were glad the cash register and the typewriters had been safely tucked away in our wardrobe,'* Anne writes in her diary.

Miep tells them that many people have begun breaking into houses – ordinary people who would never have done anything like it before. But the people of Amsterdam have very little food and clothes left, and they have no money to buy things.

Then there is good news: Radio Oranje reports that Italy has surrendered. Italy had been fighting on Germany's side, but has now joined the countries fighting against Germany.

# Food

At first the food in the secret annex was
good. Miep bought meat at a butcher
she trusted. A baker made bread for them,
and the greengrocer brought potatoes and
vegetables between 12.30 and 2.00 p.m.
when the people from the warehouse had
gone home, so the workers would not ask
why so much food was being brought in.
The people in hiding made their own
sausages from minced meat.

That first year, there was enough food,
but then it became more difficult to get food.
Their attic supplies were running low, and
Miep and Bep needed ration coupons to buy
food. Ordinary people got ration books from
the council, but of course the family in the
secret annex didn't, so the helpers had to

buy them on the black market. And the price went up week by week.

Anne wrote about one meal:

*'Lunch today is mashed potato and pickled kale. You won't believe how much kale can stink when it's a few years old. Our potatoes have contracted such strange diseases that one out of every two buckets ends up in the dustbin. We entertain ourselves trying to work out which diseases they've got and we've reached the conclusion they suffer from cancer, smallpox and measles.'*

The stove is very important in the secret annex. They use it to burn most of their rubbish. They can't simply throw things away in a bin because people working in the warehouse might ask questions if there was too much waste in the bins. So the stove burns a lot, even when it's warm.

After 18 months, the food shortage becomes serious. The man who got the ration books is arrested. The people in the

secret annex don't have much to eat.
They are hungry all day long, and that
makes them unhappy.

*The living room in the annex*

# Moods

Anne tries to keep friendly with everyone, but she often gets cross with other people living in the annex.

*'I'd like to scream, stamp my foot, give Mother a good shaking, cry and I don't know what else,'* she writes. *'I'd like to scream "leave me alone!"'*

Anne feels that no one likes her.

*'Everyone thinks I am showing off when I talk, ridiculous when I'm silent, insolent when I answer, cunning when I have a good idea, lazy when I'm tired, selfish when I eat one bite more than I should.'*

She acts as if the criticism does not bother her. She laughs it off and says 'I'm a hopeless case.' But in her diary she says she does her best to please everyone.

Sometimes she manages to be really merry. One evening Peter puts on a dress of his mother's and Anne puts on Peter's suit and cap. Everyone laughs at them.

Sometimes Anne and Margot get on well too. Then they tell each other their dreams for the future. Margot wants to nurse newborn babies in Palestine and Anne dreams of studying history of art in London and Paris.

Sometimes the eight of them dream together. They talk about the first thing they will do when they get outside again. Margot and Mr Van Pels want a hot bath. Mrs Van Pels wants to eat cakes. Anne's mother wants a cup of real coffee. Peter wants to go to the cinema. Mr Pfeffer wants to see his wife. Anne's father wants to visit Bep Voskuijl's father, who is very ill. And Anne...

*'I would be so overjoyed I would not know where to begin,'* she writes. *'Most of all, I long to have a home of our own, to move around freely and go to school again.'*

# Worries

Mr Kleiman and Mr Kugler are worried because a new person has come to work in the warehouse. He knows nothing about the people hiding in the annex, but he asks a lot of questions about the back of the house, and they think that he steals things from Opekta. He makes everyone uneasy. And the atmosphere in the annex is already tense.

Mr and Mrs Van Pels argue a lot. Their money has run out, and Mr Van Pels wants his wife to sell her fur coat. Kleiman knows a man who will pay 325 guilders for it, which is a lot of money. The Van Pels family could then help pay towards the household again.

But Mrs Van Pels does not want to sell her coat – she shouts and cries and stamps her foot. The other people living in the annex don't dare to say anything. They stand at the bottom of the stairs and hold their breath. In the end the fur coat is sold.

Anne is becoming more depressed. She looks bad. Everyone says so. She gets all sorts of pick-me-ups – grape sugar, cod-liver oil, calcium tablets, the herb valerian – but nothing helps. 'A good laugh would do me more good than all those pills,' thinks Anne. 'I need to go outside, to breathe fresh air. I am like a bird without wings in a cage which is too small.'

Anne becomes more depressed when Mrs Kleiman comes to visit. She talks about her daughter Corry: her hockey club, her school trip, the play she performed at school.

*'I long to have a really good time for once and to laugh so much that it hurts ... I long to ride a bike, dance, whistle, look at the world, feel young and know that I am free, and yet I can't let it show.'*

# Someone To Talk To

Anne's diary is a great comfort to her, but she still misses having someone to talk to – someone she can talk to about private things. One day she decides that Peter could be a good person to talk to. She knows Peter likes to do crossword puzzles so she offers to help him. It is a trick to be able to spend some time alone with him in his room. But Peter is shy and unsure; they do the crossword together but don't talk about anything else. At night, in bed, Anne is disappointed – she hates having to try so hard to make contact.

A couple of weeks later she tries again. Peter, Anne and Margot are peeling potatoes. They are talking about Moffie, the cat that lives in the main house.

'We're still not sure whether Moffie is a boy or a girl, are we?' asks Anne.

'Yes, we are,' says Peter. 'He's a tomcat. You can see for yourself.'

In the afternoon, Anne goes downstairs to where Peter is. He grabs the cat and shows him to Anne. 'See,' he says. 'This is the male sexual organ.' Then he lets the cat go. Anne is surprised that Peter talks so freely.

After this, something changes in Peter. He keeps looking at Anne:

*'Not in the usual way,'* she writes.

Sometimes Anne looks back and then...

*'It made me feel wonderful inside.'*

# A Little in Love

Anne spends as much time with Peter in his room as she can. Peter is nowhere near as shy as he used to be, and they talk about everything. Anne tells her diary she is not really in love with him, but she really likes having a friend at last. Anne's mother does not like the way Anne spends so much time with Peter and thinks Anne is bothering him – but Anne doesn't care.

Anne's life in the secret annex is better. She thinks about Peter all day long and she goes to see him whenever she can. She often sits in the attic because Peter is there. One window in the attic can open, and Anne likes to look at the blue sky and the leaves on the chestnut tree. She loves to look at the sun and the clouds. She breathes in fresh air

**Peter Van Pels**
*Anne is beginning to fall in love with Peter.*

deeply. 'As long as this exists, this sunshine and this cloudless sky, how can I be sad?' she thinks. At those moments, she feels at one with God.

Anne thinks she and Peter are the same in a lot of ways. They are both young, both unsure. They both have a mother who does not understand them. They have both been locked up for 18 months and they can't do the things that normal teenagers do: they can't go to school, go out in the evening, do sport and join clubs. That is why they get on so well.

But there is one big difference between Anne and Peter. If Anne feels unsure of herself, she gets loud, but Peter shuts himself away in his room. 'That is why I am so restless,' Anne tells Peter. 'I don't have my own room. I don't have a place of my own. I am sent from one corner to another. I can only be myself when I am with you in the attic. And in my diary, of course.'

Anne realises she is beginning to fall in love with Peter. She tries to find out what he thinks about her. One day she asks him what he would do if a dozen Annes kept popping in to see him.

'If they were all like you, it wouldn't be so bad,' Peter answers.

**Peter's room**
*Anne spends a lot of time with Peter in his room.*

# Information

Anne doesn't think her parents have told her enough about sex.

*'Instead of telling their sons and daughters everything at the age of 12, they send the children out of the room the moment the subject comes up,'* she writes in her diary.

Anne thinks she knows why. She thinks they are worried their children will no longer want to wait until marriage.

*'This purity is a lot of nonsense,'* she writes. *'As far as I am concerned, it's not wrong for a man to bring a little experience to a marriage.'*

When she was 11, Anne's parents told her about periods, but they did not tell her what it meant. Anne knew how a baby came to be in a woman's tummy, but she did not know how it came out. Her friend Jacqueline told her more, but Anne is still confused. She wonders if Peter will answer some of her questions.

She asks Peter about how to stop getting pregnant and he explains it to her, but she still has some doubts. 'How do you know when a boy is grown up?' she asks Peter. 'I will tell you tonight,' Peter promises.

Anne is a bit embarrassed when Peter tells her about boys, but Peter is very normal and open.

*'Neither he nor I had ever imagined we'd be able to talk so openly to a girl or boy about such intimate matters,'* Anne writes. *'I think I know everything now.'*

# Peter

The adults are curious. 'What do you two talk about all the time?' they ask Anne and Peter. But they say nothing.

*'Imagine they knew,'* writes Anne. *'It is unusual to talk about things like periods with a boy. And a boy who talks about his things with a girl is unusual as well.'*

Anne knows that Peter does not know a lot about girls, and she wants to tell him what a girl looks like.

*'I don't think boys are as complicated as girls,'* she writes. *'You can easily see what boys look like, but with women it's different.'*

Anne practises in her diary how she will describe a girl to Peter.

The adults keep on making their irritating jokes, but Anne does not understand why.

**Peter with his friends**
*Peter Van Pels (middle) with his friends in Germany, around 1936.*

*'It is enough just being together,'* she writes. *'Often we don't talk about anything.'*

Anne's mother bans her from spending so much time with Peter. She thinks Peter is in love with Anne and she does not want Anne to encourage him. But Anne does not want to give Peter up – and she hopes he is in love with her.

*'I so long for a kiss,'* she writes in her diary. But the kiss doesn't come.

Then something terrible happens. There is another burglary – and this time they are all in grave danger.

# The Break-in

It is the evening of Easter Sunday. They hear a few loud bangs in the warehouse and the men go to look. They surprise two burglars, who run off. The burglars have taken a panel off the wooden door to get in. The men put the plank back against the door, but the burglars return and it is easy for them to push the plank out again.

Mr Van Pels gets angry, bangs on the floor with an axe and shouts 'Police!' The burglars run off again, but a man and woman who are walking along the street see the men running away. They shine their torch through the hole in the door.

The men go upstairs to Mr and Mrs Van Pels's room, where the women are waiting there in a nervous group. They think the

couple on the street will tell the police.
The police can arrive at any moment, so
the people in hiding have to keep very quiet.
Not a single noise can come from upstairs.

Later that evening they hear noises. There
are footsteps in the house, in the office, in
the kitchen downstairs. Someone rattles
the bookcase. 'Now we are done for,' thinks
Anne. But the footsteps fade away.

They are all shaking with fear and have to
use the toilet, but of course, no one can use
it. The only thing they can do is use Peter's
waste-paper bin. After a while, it starts to
really smell.

The next day someone phones Mr Kleiman.
He warns Miep and her husband Jan, and
they come to the annex straight away.

'I've been to the police,' says Jan, 'but they
don't know anything about it. But then I met
the greengrocer. I told him there had been
a break-in. He said he knew because he and
his wife were the couple who saw the hole by

the light of their torch. He said he had not told the police and that he did not know anything, but that he had his suspicions.'

**Johannes Kleiman and Victor Kugler after the war**
*While the people were hiding in the annex, the two men did everything they could to help them.*

# Is This Okay?

*'That night I really thought I was going
to die,'* writes Anne after the break-in.
*'I waited for the police and I was ready for
death, like a soldier. But now, now that
I've been spared, my first wish after the
war is to become a Dutch citizen. I love
the Dutch, I love this country. And even
if I have to write to the Queen herself, I
won't give up until I've reached my goal.'*
She writes a lot about Peter as well.
They've been sitting close together among
the junk in the attic. They've put their arms
around each other's shoulders, and looked
outside through the attic window at the
birds, at the chestnut tree and the blue sky.
Anne is happy because she has finally had
that kiss she longed for.

**A page from Anne's diary**
*Anne writes about her feelings and about what she thinks of her world.*

Anne is now really in love. When she is
with Peter they sit so close together. They
don't talk much any more.

*'It's so thrilling to feel his cheek against
mine,'* she writes.

And she asks herself if it is okay to do this.
Perhaps Peter will want to go further. Should
she stop him? She thinks her friends would
be shocked. But she thinks differently. They

are stuck inside, frightened and worried –
why should she have to wait until she is old
enough? Why should she not make herself
and Peter happy?

The relationship becomes more serious.
One evening they kiss full on the mouth.

*'In a daze, we embraced,'* Anne writes.

She still has doubts. Is it right for a girl
to do this? Can she have as much passion
as Peter?

*'There is only one possible answer,'* she
writes. *'I'm longing so much ... and have
for such a long time. I'm so lonely and
now I've found comfort.'*

**The chestnut tree in 2007**
*If Anne and Peter look through the attic window they see the chestnut tree.*

# A Journalist and Writer

Mr Bolkestein, a Dutch government minister, said on the radio that after the war a collection would be made of diaries and letters written about the war. Anne and the others in the secret annex think it's a great idea, and they think Anne's diary would be perfect.

*'Ten years after the war it will be very amusing to read how we lived,'* writes Anne. *'How we lived, what we ate and what we talked about as Jews in hiding.'*

After the minister's speech, Anne starts to think.

*'For a long time now I didn't know why I was bothering to do any school work. The end of the war still seemed so far away.'*

But now Anne thinks differently. She is doing her school work so she can become a journalist.

*'I can't imagine having to live like mother and Mrs Van Pels, who go about their work and then are forgotten. I need to have something as well as a husband and children. I want to go on living even after my death.'*

But Anne does not just want to be a journalist – she wants to be a famous writer. And after the war she will publish a book called *The Secret Annex.*

*'I can use my diary as a start,'* she writes.

She uses loose pieces of paper to re-write parts of her diary. She writes some pieces all over again, and she leaves other bits out because she thinks they are childish or too private.

# The Letter

Anne decides to talk to her father about Peter. When they are alone she tells him: 'Father, when Peter and I are together we don't exactly sit at opposite ends of the room. Do you think that's wrong?'

At first Anne's father says he doesn't think it's wrong, but the next day he tells Anne she should not go upstairs so often. 'In matters like these it is always the man who takes the active role and it's up to the woman to set the limits,' he says. He wants her to stay away from the attic. But Anne does not want to do what her father says.

*'I like being with Peter and I trust him,'* she writes. *'No, I'm going to the attic.'*

Anne's father is unhappy with her. He thought she would listen to him but she doesn't. Anne feels bad as well because her father is cross with her and she writes him an angry letter. She says she only told him because she did not want him to think she was doing things behind his back. She says she knows herself what she can and can't do. She says she has been alone for years and no one helps her with her problems. She says she has had to do everything herself. She says he can't treat her like a child – she may only be 14 but all the troubles have made her older. She puts the letter in her father's pocket.

Her father is very upset by the letter. 'I've received many letters in my lifetime, but none as hurtful as this,' he tells her. 'You who have had so much love from your parents. No, Anne. We did not deserve this.'

Anne is very sorry about what she has done. *I used my tears to show off,'* she writes. *'It's good that somebody has finally cut me down to size. I'll take Father as an example once again and I will improve myself.'*

**Otto Frank**
*Anne is very sorry about the letter she wrote to her father.*

# Troubles

Anne is very shocked: the greengrocer has been arrested. He had two Jews in his house.

*'The world's been turned upside down,'* she writes. *'The most decent people are being sent to concentration camps and the lowest of the low rule over young and old, rich and poor.'*

They will miss the greengrocer. Now they will have less to eat – no more breakfast, only porridge with bread for lunch and fried potatoes in the evening.

Anne knows their helpers run big risks. *'They have an enormous responsibility for the eight of us,'* she writes. *'I've asked myself again and again whether it wouldn't have been better if we hadn't gone into hiding, if we were dead now and didn't*

*have to go through this misery, especially
so the others could be spared this burden.'*

Anne also has her worries about Peter. He
is not the person she thought he was. Once
he said that after the war he might become a
criminal. She knows it was a joke but still...

And she sees that Peter wants an easy
life – he even said he would rather not be a
Jew. That hurt Anne. She thinks it is very
important to be Jewish.

*'We can never be just Dutch or just English,
or whatever. We will always be Jews too.'*

**The annex kitchen**
*This is where meals were cooked. It got more and more difficult for the
helpers to buy food for the people in hiding.*

# The Invasion

'This is D-Day,' says the radio announcer.
At last, the invasion is happening. Anne and
the others have been waiting for this for a
long time. 156,000 English, American and
Canadian soldiers have landed on the
French coast and are fighting the Germans.

Everyone in the secret annex is excited. Will
1944 be the great victory? Will there finally
be an end to the war? Anne thinks that by
September she may be able to go to school.

Anne has her second birthday in the annex.
She is now 15. She gets books, underwear
and nice things to eat: yoghurt, a pot of jam,
two small honey biscuits and three pieces of
cheese. Peter gives her a big bunch of peonies
that Miep had bought for him. Anne is very
happy with all the presents.

A month later, there is more good news: a young German officer tried to kill Hitler. Sadly, it did not work.

Anne thinks a lot about Peter. She knows she made Peter like her. She wanted a friend and she made him the perfect one, and he finally had feelings for her.

*'We talked about the most private things,'* she writes. *'But when I think about it now, it seems outrageous. I used intimacy to get close to him and now I can see he is beginning to like me more with each passing day.'*

But she thinks she forced Peter to get close to her and now he won't let go. She would like to shake him off again. Anne still has problems with the adults in the annex.

*'If I am quiet and serious, everyone thinks I'm putting on an act.'*

So she laughs and pretends to be cheerful. Anne wants to be different. She wants people to see that she can be serious.

# Betrayed

Friday, 4 August begins like any other day.
People are working in the office and the
warehouse. In the secret annex the people in
hiding are quietly going about their business.
It is a fine, warm summer's day.

At 10.30 a.m. a car stops suddenly on the
Prinsengracht, right in front of number 263.
Three Dutch policemen get out with an SS
officer in charge. They go straight into the
Opekta warehouse.

Someone has phoned the German
police and told them there are Jews hiding
there. The people hiding in the annex have
been betrayed.

The officers open the bookcase door and
go into the annex, their pistols out. Everyone
is put in one room. The SS officer picks up

Anne's father's bag and empties it. Anne's diary, her notebooks and the loose sheets of paper she had written on fall to the ground. The officers look for all the jewellery and order everyone outside. First they are allowed to pack a bag.

Johannes Kleiman and Victor Kugler are arrested as well. The officers leave Miep Gies alone. Bep Voskuijl was quickly sent away by

**The warehouse**
*On 4 August 1944 SS officer Karl Silberbauer and his men entered the building through this door.*

Mr Kleiman and had not been stopped by the officers. Anne's father thinks it is terrible that Mr Kleiman and Mr Kugler are being taken away as well, but Kleiman calms him down. He says he is not sorry about helping the family.

Once Anne and the others are gone, Miep and Bep go into the secret annex. The Germans have searched everywhere for jewellery and money. Anne's diary lies on the ground. They pick up all the papers and Miep puts them in the drawer of her desk.

A few days later the secret annex is emptied. Things that belonged to the Jews who have been taken prisoner are often sent to Germany, where they are given away to German families.

# Taken Away

After spending more than two years indoors, Anne and the others are now outside. It is terrible to have been arrested, but Anne enjoys the fresh air. On the train on their way to the Westerbork transit camp she looks outside all the time, at the fields, at the corn growing. She has missed it all for so long.

At Westerbork they are placed in a separate part of the prison – they are being punished because they had gone into hiding. Jews who turned themselves in to the SS are treated better. Anne, Margot and their mother are placed in a barracks for women. Anne's father is in the men's barracks, but is allowed to visit sometimes.

It is strange to think it, but Anne is happy in Westerbork. It is not nice in the camp, but

**Muiderpoort railway station in Amsterdam, May 1943**
*Jewish children and their parents wait for the train to take them to the Westerbork camp.*

she is still pleased. She sees new people and likes to talk to them. Her parents are very quiet – they are frightened that the family will be sent to the concentration camps in Eastern Europe. No one really knows what happens there, but everyone fears the worst.

On 2 September all eight people from the secret annex are on the list, and have to take the train east the next day.

More than 1,000 people are crammed into the train. There is no toilet and they have to use a bucket, which starts to smell. The carriages are overcrowded. There is no room to sit down. Anne and Margot are lucky – they can lean on their parents.

Some prisoners have hidden money and jewellery under their clothes, but the German soldiers find it and take it away.

The train takes a long time – three days and nights. Sometimes it stops and the prisoners are allowed to get off. They can have something to drink and empty the smelly bucket, but then the journey continues and the bucket starts to smell again.

Then the train stops one last time. They are in Auschwitz, the big Polish extermination camp. The Nazis rule Poland as well.

The prisoners have to leave their bags on the train. Women have to stand on one side, men on the other. It is the last time that Anne's father will see his wife and daughters.

'I will never forget the look in Margot's eyes,' he later says.

# Auschwitz

Nazi doctors check all the prisoners one
by one. Old people and mothers with small
children go one way; they are taken straight
into the gas chambers.

The gas chambers look like shower rooms,
but no water comes out of the shower heads.
Instead, a deadly gas comes out of holes
in the ceiling. The prisoners don't know
that – they think they are going to shower.
Everyone has to undress and go into the
shower room. After a little while, they are
all dead and their bodies are all over the
ground. Other prisoners have to take the
bodies to be burned.

The men and women who do not go
to the gas chambers have to have a real
shower. They have to undress and their hair

is shaved off, then a number is tattooed on their arms.

It is a hard life in Auschwitz. For example, they have to carry rocks and stand for hours in the cold so they can be counted. They get very little to eat: cabbage soup and a piece of bread. The washing areas and toilets are dirty.

Many prisoners become ill but they don't get any medicine and some become too sick to work. They are sent to the gas chambers. The flames of the crematorium can be seen all day and all night. Bodies are being burned there all the time.

Anne's father, Mr Van Pels, Peter and Mr Pfeffer are in the men's camp, where, for example, they have to dig ditches all day long. One day Mr Van Pels hurts his thumb. That will be his death. He can't work and has to stay in the barracks, but every day the Germans check the barracks, and people who can't work are murdered.

Peter and Otto Frank see Mr Van Pels being taken away with other prisoners. Two hours later a lorry returns, carrying only clothes. Mr Van Pels is the first of the eight people from the secret annex to die.

# Leaving Auschwitz

In the meantime, Russian soldiers are moving deeper into Poland. The German army has to retreat, so the Nazis decide to move the prisoners away from Auschwitz. All the women who can still work are sent back to Germany. Nazi doctors decide which women can stand the long journey back.

Anne, Margot and their mother are checked – one by one they have to stand naked under a strong light. It is the last time Anne's mother sees her daughters. She has to stay in Auschwitz while Anne and Margot are put on the train back to Germany.

The train trip to the Bergen-Belsen concentration camp takes three days. It's a terrible journey – many prisoners are starving and die on the way.

Anne and Margot survive the journey but it is not much better in Bergen-Belsen. The barracks are too full so they have to sleep in a tent. It is cold, but when the tent blows down, they are allowed to sleep in the barracks. There are far too many women sleeping in them.

It is hard to survive in the winter of 1944–45. The prisoners get very little food; sometimes they get nothing at all. There are outbreaks of illness. Anne and Margot try to stay hopeful. In December 1944 they celebrate Hanukkah, St Nicholas and Christmas with some other women, all in one go. They sing songs and eat a celebration meal of old bread, a little onion and cooked cabbage. They have been saving up the bread for days. For a few hours they almost forget their troubles.

In Auschwitz it is even colder. Sometimes it freezes to 40 degrees below zero. Anne's mother falls ill and dies in January 1945.

# An Old Friend

The Russian army is getting closer and the Nazis are nervous – Auschwitz has to be empty before the Russians come. The Nazis flee. The gas chambers and the crematorium are blown up with dynamite. The Russian soldiers must not be able to guess what happened in Auschwitz.

All the prisoners who can walk have to go with the German soldiers. Peter Van Pels is one of them, but Anne's father is too weak and stays behind. The guards want to shoot the people who are left behind but there is not enough time for that – the Russians are almost at the gates. The last Germans leave Auschwitz in a hurry.

On 27 January 1945, the Russian army arrives at Auschwitz. Anne's father is

**Auschwitz-Birkenau**
*The camp shortly after it was liberated by the Russians.*

freed. He is one of only 7,650 people
still alive.

Mrs Van Pels has been taken to Bergen-
Belsen, where she meets Anne and Margot.
Later she is moved to another part of the
camp and there she meets an old friend of
Anne's, Hanneli.

Hanneli is very surprised Anne is in
Bergen-Belsen – the whole war long she
thought Anne had escaped to another
country. Hanneli wants to go to Anne but
she can't because the different parts of the

camp are separated by barbed wire and high bales of straw.

Hanneli and Anne do manage to talk a few times, although they can't see each other. Anne says her head has been shaved and she is very thin.

Hanneli is a bit better off and next time she brings some food and clothes for Anne. She throws the parcel over the bales of straw but then she hears Anne crying and screaming. Another prisoner has grabbed the parcel.

The next time Hanneli brings another parcel for Anne, and this time Anne does get the food and the clothes.

The contact between Anne and her old friend does not last long because Anne has to move to another barracks. She can no longer get to the wall of barbed wire and straw.

# The End

Life in Bergen-Belsen gets harder. There is little to eat and lots of disease. Anne's clothes are covered with lice and fleas. She thinks it is so horrible she throws all her clothes away and has only a blanket to wrap around herself. Another prisoner finds clothes for Anne. It is winter and very cold.

Margot and Anne become ill. They have a high temperature and rash – typhoid. They got the illness from the lice. They stay in bed in the ice-cold barracks; they have no warm clothes and shiver all the time.

Every time the door opens, it gets colder. 'Shut the door!' they shout. Their beds are close to the entrance and they are too weak to get up and close the door themselves.

One day Margot falls out of bed on to the stone floor. She can't get up again, and dies. Shortly thereafter, Anne dies too. They have been together throughout the entire war. Their bodies are thrown on a big pile of other dead bodies. It is March 1945.

On 15 April, the camp is liberated by English soldiers. The soldiers are shocked by what they find – there are bodies everywhere. They dig deep graves for the thousands of dead, and they burn down the barracks to make sure the diseases do not spread.

**Prisoners who have been freed at Bergen-Belsen**
*Liberation came too late for Anne and Margot.*

# Back to Amsterdam

Their father has been free for weeks when Anne and Margot die, but he is still too weak to make the trip back to the Netherlands. By the end of March he is strong enough to travel.

The journey back to the Netherlands takes a long time. Anne's father has to go a long way round because there is still fighting in many parts of Europe. First he goes to Russia and then takes a boat to France. On the way he meets a woman who has survived Auschwitz who tells him his wife has died, but he hears nothing about his daughters. He hopes to see them again in Amsterdam.

On 3 June 1945, Anne's father arrives in Amsterdam. He goes straight to see Miep and Jan Gies.

They are very happy to see him again, but they have heard nothing about Anne and Margot. They tell him about the other helpers. Mr Kugler and Mr Kleiman were in prison but are now back with their families. Bep Voskuijl is also well. But Mr Pfeffer, Mrs Van Pels and Peter Van Pels were killed in the concentration camps.

Anne's father tries to find out what has happened to his daughters. He puts an advert in the newspaper. He writes letters to all sorts of organisations. He talks to people returning from other concentration camps. Finally he meets two sisters who were in Bergen-Belsen, who tell him about Anne and Margot's terrible last days and the way they died.

# Anne's Diary

Anne's father tells the sad news to Miep. She goes straight away to the drawer of her desk. 'This is what your daughter has left you,' she says. She gives him the diary, the notebooks and the loose pieces of paper.

Anne's father can't read the diary straight away – he is too sad. Weeks later he begins to read, a few pages at a time. He is very moved by it and he sees that he did not know his daughter very well.

'This was a very different Anne to the one I knew,' he says later. 'I had no idea of the depths of her thoughts and feelings.'

Anne's father decides to publish the diary because that was what Anne wanted to do. He tries to find a publisher but it is not easy – people don't want to read about all the misery so soon after the war has ended. They would rather forget.

Anne's diary is finally published two years after the war. It is given the name she thought up herself – *The Secret Annex.*

The book becomes very popular and is sold out very quickly. Everyone likes it. There is a new printing and another and another. The diary is turned into films and plays. And the secret hiding place becomes a museum.

Millions of people all over the world know who Anne Frank was. An ordinary girl who was unlucky to be Jewish. An ordinary girl who was unlucky that Hitler became leader of Germany. An ordinary girl who was unlucky that someone knew about the secret annex and betrayed the people hiding there.

But one thing about Anne was not ordinary: she could write very well.

# Who Betrayed Them?

Everyone wants to know who betrayed the people in hiding: Anne's father wanted to know; Miep and her husband wanted to know; the other people who helped the family wanted to know.

They all tried to find out who it was, but nobody really knows.

Later, Anne's father said it did not really matter any more. 'What happened, happened and nothing can change that,' he said. 'It is more important that we learn something from it.'

But other people don't agree with him. Many of them have looked at old files and papers, and some of them think they know the answer.

Some people say it was a man from the warehouse. Some say it was the woman who cleaned the Prinsengracht office. Some say it was a friend of Anne's father.

But there is no proof – it could easily be someone else. We will probably never know.

*Anne's diary papers*
*Some of the diary papers that Miep Gies handed over to Otto.*

# Afterword

This was the story of Anne Frank. This was the story of the 1.5 million Jewish children murdered during the Second World War.

Anne has become famous all over the world because of her diary. Millions of people all over the world have read it.

Anne's father got many letters about Anne, especially from young people. They wanted to know how something so terrible could happen. Otto Frank answered all the letters. In an interview he once said: 'I answer them as well as I can. And at the end I finish by saying, "I hope that Anne's book will have an effect on the rest of your life. So that you will work for unity and peace."'

# Word List

**Adolf Hitler**

Adolf Hitler was the leader of the Nazi Party in Germany. In 1933 he became chancellor, or leader of the government. Germany quickly turned into a dictatorship: what Hitler and his party wanted, had to happen. Hitler was one of the twentieth century's cruellest dictators. He wanted Germany to be lived in by healthy Germans with blonde hair and blue eyes. People who were different were arrested and often killed.

**Auschwitz**

Auschwitz was a big concentration camp in Poland run by the Nazis. Poland was occupied by the German army as well. Almost every day trains with Jewish prisoners arrived at Auschwitz. The Nazis' aim was to either kill everyone in the gas chambers or make them work so hard that they died of exhaustion or disease.

**barracks**

A barracks is a big, empty shed. People in concentration camps slept in barracks.

**concentration camps**

Jews who were arrested were taken to concentration camps, which were big prisons. Prisoners did not get much to eat and had to work hard. The Nazis killed a lot of Jews in concentration camps.

**crematorium**

A crematorium is a place where bodies are burned. The extermination camps built by the Germans had large crematoriums to get rid of the bodies of the people who had been killed in the gas chambers or who had died from disease.

**crisis**

A crisis is an emergency situation. At times of crisis there are many problems.

**D-Day**

D-Day is the day that the American, British and Canadian soldiers landed by ship on the French coast. They came to fight the Germans.

**dictator**

A dictator has all the power in a country. He decides what will happen.

**extermination camp**

The Nazis built lots of concentration camps in Eastern Europe. Some of them were extermination camps, built to kill as many people as possible.

**Hanukkah**

Hanukkah is the Jewish festival of light. Jewish people burn candles in a special candle holder. You begin with one candle and every day you add another. After eight days, all the candles are burning. While the candles burn people sing songs and children get presents.

**Jews**

Many Jews practise the Jewish religion. The Jewish religion is very old and was one of the first to have a single god.

**laws for the Jews**

Hitler's government introduced lots of different laws for Jews. The aim of these laws was to keep Jews out of normal society.

## Nazis

The Nazis were Hitler's supporters. They are most famous for their hatred of the Jews, but the Nazis also hated other groups of people like Roma and Sinti, homosexuals, people with handicaps and Jehovah's Witnesses.

## Radio Oranje

During the war, the Dutch liked to listen to English radio. The BBC broadcast a special programme for the Netherlands called Radio Oranje. Britain was not occupied by the Nazis so the news was 'real'. In the Netherlands, the radio stations broadcast the news that the Nazis wanted. The Dutch Queen Wilhelmina often spoke on Radio Oranje to give the Dutch hope. Listening to Radio Oranje was banned, and if you were caught, you would be arrested.

## rumour

A rumour is a story that may or may not be true.

## SS

The SS (*Schutzstaffel*) was a group of specially trained German soldiers. Many people were afraid of the SS because they could be very cruel.

**sugar ration cards**

During the war there was not much to eat, so the government gave out rations, not just for food but also for clothes and shoes. That way everything was shared fairly. You could only buy sugar if you had a sugar ration card.

**surrendered**

Stopped fighting. Italy was on the side of Germany, so it was good news for the people in hiding when the Italians surrendered because it meant Germany had one less ally.

**Westerbork transit camp**

Jews who were arrested in the Netherlands were taken first to the Westerbork transit camp in Drenthe. From there they were taken to the concentration camps in Eastern Europe. In total, 107,000 Jewish Dutch people were taken to concentration camps. Just 5,000 survived.